SCENES ALONG THE LINE OF
THE SAN JOSE & LOS GATOS
INTERURBAN RAILROAD

PHOTOGRAPHS BY ANDREW P. HILL

SCENES ALONG THE LINE
OF
THE SAN JOSE & LOS GATOS
INTERURBAN RAILROAD

PHOTOGRAPHS BY
ANDREW P. HILL

THIS LIMITED EDITION WAS PRINTED IN 1994 AS A MEMBERSHIP PREMIUM BY THE
SAN JOSE HISTORICAL MUSEUM ASSOCIATION
1650 SENTER ROAD
SAN JOSE, CALIFORNIA 95112

Printed in U.S.A. by
The Rosicrucian Press
76 Notre Dame Avenue
San Jose, CA 95113

Design and layout by
Digital Typography & Design
2925 Varden Avenue
San Jose, CA 95124-1673

Limited first edition, 1994
Published by the San Jose Historical Museum Association

FOREWORD

$\mathscr{I}$t is with great pleasure that the San Jose Historical Museum Association publishes this volume of photographs taken by noted local artist and photographer Andrew P. Hill. It is always exciting when we can reproduce original materials from the Museum's collections and make them available for the enrichment of today's audience.

This particular project affords us the opportunity to shed some light on the important work of Andrew P. Hill as well as to emphasize the extensive system of early transportation lines that crisscrossed the Santa Clara Valley.

The original photo album entitled "Scenes Along the Line of the San Jose and Los Gatos Interurban Railroad" was a gift to the San Jose Historical Museum Archives in 1990 from Mr. Robert Lee Williams of Ohio. It appears to have belonged to his parents, Charles Adolf Williams and Dorothy Dietsch Williams. Mr. Williams does not know how it came to be in his family's collection.

The album has a black leather cover with gold stamped lettering. It has 24 pages and photographs are mounted on both sides of each page. Short captions were written in white ink under each photograph.

The inside cover notes "Photographs by Andrew P. Hill @ San Jose, Cal." Although there is no date anywhere in the album, it apparently was presented to the Chamber of Commerce by the San Jose and Los Gatos Interurban Railway Company at the time the Railway was constructed in 1904.

It was the decision of the Publications Committee of the Museum Association to reprint all 48 photographs in the album exactly as they appear in the original. This decision was made despite the fact our research showed that many of the photographs in the album were actually not taken along the route of the Interurban!

Included are many photographs of other subjects, such as the photographer's prized poultry, and images of geographical areas remote from the railroad route. Many of the photographs in the album also appeared previously in *Sunshine, Fruit & Flowers,* a publication of the *San Jose Mercury* issued in 1895 and revised in 1896.

Members of the Publications Committee researched each of the photographs in the album in an effort to include additional information for today's reader. Wherever possible we have pin-pointed the location of the photo in the accompanying text and on the map of the Railroad route.

This publication is, in fact, a result of the efforts of many people. The Publication Committee included volunteers Linda Larson Boston, Frances Fox, Virginia Hammerness, Charles Hopkins, Helen Kuesel, Patricia Loomis, Julia O'Keefe, Earline Shields, Judge Mark Thomas, Jr., and William Wulf. San Jose Historical Museum Archivist Leslie Masunaga generously provided the original album and her expertise in identifying many of the photographs. Trolley Barn Manager Fred Bennett identified photographs as well, and drew the map of the Interurban route that appears in this publication. Association staff member Kindra Donald researched and helped write the introductory pieces on Andrew P. Hill and the Interurban Railroad. Administrative Assistant Judi Henderson provided invaluable assistance at every stage of the production.

Publication of *Scenes Along the Line of the San Jose and Los Gatos Interurban Railroad* was made possible through generous grants from the Stella B. Gross Charitable Trust and the Sourisseau Academy of San Jose State University.

Kathleen Muller
Editor

ANDREW P. HILL

Andrew Putnam Hill age 37.

Scenes Along the Line of the San Jose and Los Gatos Interurban Railroad was designed to give the reader a look through the lens of the naturalist artist and conservationist, Andrew Putnam Hill.

Born in Porter County, Indiana on August 9, 1853, Hill was the only child of Elijah and Jane Hill. Both of Andrew's parents were descendants of colonial Americans. At the age of fourteen, Andrew traveled with his uncle to California where he attended Santa Clara College. For a year Hill studied in the equivalent of the high school department, followed by a year at the secondary level. Having fostered a love for nature and the art of expressing it, Hill enrolled in the California School of Design in San Francisco in 1875.

In 1876 Hill went into partnership with Louis Lussier and opened a portrait painting business in San Jose where the two worked together to paint, among other subjects, life-size portraits of many political figures. Perhaps the most popular painting that emerged from this partnership was that entitled, "The Murphy Party." This large painting depicted the first wagon party of settlers to conquer Sunset Pass in the Sierra Nevadas. The painting was purchased by the California Pioneers Association and hung in their historical room in San Francisco until it was destroyed in the 1906 earthquake and fire. After the death of Lussier in 1882, Hill worked alone in a studio on North First Street.

In April 1883, Hill married Florence Maria Watkins, a local Santa Claran by birth. The Hill's first child, a son, was born on February 6, 1884. Three days later he died. On June 4, 1886, a second son, Andrew Putnam, Jr. was born and would survive to carry on his father's name. A third son, Frank Ernest, was born on August 29, 1888.

In 1889 Mr. Hill formed a partnership with J.C. Franklin and together they operated the Hill and Franklin Photography Studio and Art Gallery. Franklin left the business after only one year. Hill then entered a partnership with his mother-in-law, Laura Broughton Watkins and established the Hill and Watkins Photographers Studio. In 1892 Sidney Yard, artist and photographer, joined the studio and stayed for three years. During this time the partners exhibited their work, among other

Andrew Hill's studio late 1890's.

places, at the World's Columbian Exposition in Chicago in 1893.

After Yard left the partnership, Hill continued his painting and photography from a studio in the Dougherty Building. Both the studio and Hill's works were destroyed in the 1906 earthquake. Hill did not reopen his business after this disaster, but rather operated, unsuccessfully from San Jose, a gold mine in Calaveras County. He did continue to paint and photograph, but he worked out of his home on Sherman Street.

Andrew Hill first became involved in the campaign to "Save the Redwoods" of Big Basin when he was commissioned by an English publication, *Wide World Magazine,* to photograph the aftermath of a forest fire in the Santa Cruz Mountains put out with wine from a nearby winery. His attempts to photograph the area were thwarted by a land owner who told Hill the "trees were destined to become firewood and railroad ties."

On the evening of May 18, 1900, while camping among the redwoods with other conservation-minded citizens, Hill suggested the development of a forest club whose mission would include the preservation of Big Basin. The others agreed and the Sempervirens Club of California was born.

The first major decision made by the Club was that Big Basin should be purchased as a public park. Since relatively no cash existed in the treasury of the Sempervirens Club, it was proposed that the legislature be asked for the necessary funding. A bill was drafted by a Semperviren, Charles Reed, and introduced to the legislature by Assemblyman George H. Fisk of San Francisco. Father Kenna, President of Santa Clara College and a friend and supporter of Hill was able to convince the Catholic members of the legislature, who constituted a majority of the decision makers, to pass the bill. Against political opposition, mainly the supporters of logging interests, Governor Gage signed the bill and it became effective in March 1901.

To the satisfaction of the members of the Sempervirens Club, Big Basin State Park opened to campers in 1904. Hill spent his summers there and continued to photograph the magnificent redwoods until his death in 1922. To this date, the incredible redwoods still attract people of all ages and will continue to do so well into the future, due in large part, to the efforts of Andrew Hill and the Sempervirens Club.

Andrew Hill's legacies can still be enjoyed today: his paintings, his photography, and "his" redwoods. Andrew Hill captured on canvas and through the camera's eye, the evolution of California from the rush for gold to the prosperity of the early twentieth-century.

Andrew Hill camping in his beloved redwoods c. 1920.

THE SAN JOSE AND LOS GATOS INTERURBAN RAILROAD

At the turn of the century San Jose watched as other California cities prepared to welcome new interurban railroad systems. The city looked at its own run-down traction system, the San Jose Street Railway, a narrow-gauge line to Alum Rock Park and Santa Clara, and longed for its own "new century" interurban railroad system.

In the fall of 1902 the situation began to change. A consortium of local citizens headed by ex-Railroad Commissioner James W. Rea and F. S. Granger decided to form a company, the San Jose, Saratoga, and Los Gatos Interurban Railroad Company, and build and operate an electric trolley line between the three towns.

The company was incorporated on October 17, 1902. Enthusiasm ran high, but unfortunately, the financial pledges did not. Even though the corporation had entered in agreements with the County of Santa Clara to use county roads as the railroad's right-of-way and construction had begun, the project was halted due to lack of funds.

Not willing to give up, the partners reorganized and reincorporated as the San Jose and Los Gatos Interurban Railroad Company in early 1903. Realizing they would need outside funds to construct the line, they were able to secure $500,000 worth of bonds from the Germania Trust Company in St. Louis, Missouri.

Now financially able, the company resumed construction of the railroad line in June 1903. Moving quickly, the poles were erected and the electric lines were strung. The tracks, which would exit San Jose on San Carlos Street, travel down Stevens Creek Boulevard to Meridian Corners, and proceed south on Saratoga Avenue to Saratoga and Los Gatos, were soon laid. The ballast for the tracks was creek gravel from Los Gatos Creek.

In February 1904, twelve dark green cars arrived from St. Louis. Able to travel at 30 miles per hour, the cars' first trip was eagerly awaited. Four of the motor cars were named *Rea, Granger, Edith,* and *Florence* after the partners and their wives. Even the trust company was honored; one of the cars was named *Germania*.

The car barn for the line was located on the southeast corner of Sunol and San Carlos Streets. Power for the operation of the system came from a transmission line of the California Gas and Electric Company at the Otterson Street station of the United Gas and Electric Company. The railroad also maintained an electrical substation between the Fruitdale and Saratoga stations.

The inaugural trip was made on March 19, 1904. A banquet, at the end of the line in Los Gatos at the Lyndon Hotel, culminated the trip. Regular hourly service began the following week.

Rea and Granger's involvement in the line was short lived. They sold the San Jose and Los Gatos Interurban Railroad to Southern Pacific Railroad in April 1904. Oliver A. Hale became the president of the company.

The San Jose and Los Gatos Interurban Railroad was mainly a passenger line, but it did haul fruit during the canning season. The line was successful and well utilized. It remained in operation until 1938 when all the trolley lines in San Jose were abandoned.

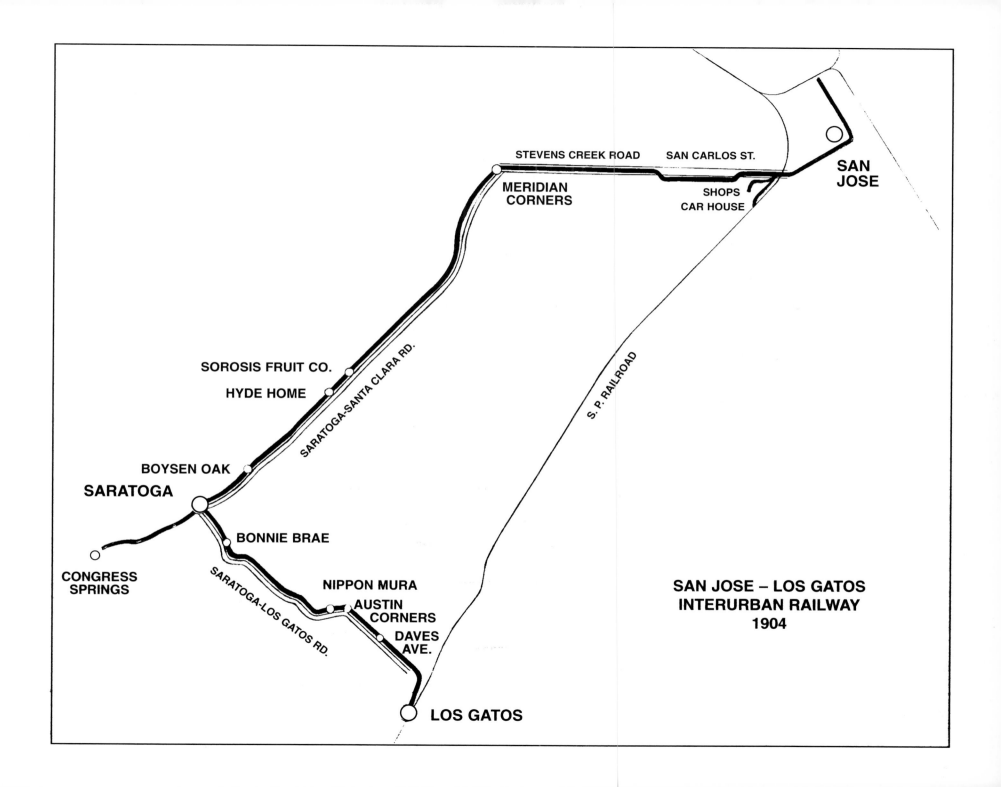

STEVENS CREEK ROAD   SAN CARLOS ST.

SAN JOSE

MERIDIAN
CORNERS

SHOPS
CAR HOUSE

SOROSIS FRUIT CO.

HYDE HOME

SARATOGA-SANTA CLARA RD.

S. P. RAILROAD

BOYSEN OAK

SARATOGA

BONNIE BRAE

CONGRESS
SPRINGS

SARATOGA-LOS GATOS RD.

NIPPON MURA

AUSTIN
CORNERS

DAVES
AVE.

**SAN JOSE – LOS GATOS
INTERURBAN RAILWAY
1904**

LOS GATOS

SCENES ALONG THE LINE

OF

THE SAN JOSE & LOS GATOS

INTERURBAN RAILROAD

PHOTOGRAPHS BY

ANDREW P. HILL

PRESENTED TO

SAN JOSE CHAMBER

OF COMMERCE

BY THE COMPANY

Photograph of actual album cover.

The photograph is of the San Jose and Los Gatos line car #101 stringing wire along Saratoga Avenue. The stringing was done from 1903 to early 1904. The car was built by the Hammond Car Company in 1891 and served in San Francisco and San Mateo as a passenger car before coming to San Jose. Upon arrival, car #101 was modified by the San Jose and Los Gatos Interurban Railway Company to serve as a stringer and line maintenance car.

San Jose, Los Gatos and Saratoga Interurban R. R.

$\mathcal{T}$his photograph was taken on Saratoga Avenue in Saratoga looking towards San Jose. It is possibly a photograph of Oliver Ambrose Hale, a financial backer of the San Jose and Los Gatos Interurban Railroad and later president of the company, and his family. Note the carriage.

During the last decade of the nineteenth century pneumatic or solid rubber tires and wooden or wire spoked wheels were adapted, first to the sulky, then to other carriages, including the surrey. The surrey in the photograph has either pneumatic or solid rubber tires and wire spoked wheels. Surreys of this period could have standing tops, falling tops, umbrella tops, removable tops, or no tops at all. Carriage bodies were painted either dark green or dark blue and had fine stripings of cream, red or black, or a combination of these colors.

Workmen on the line of the Interurban Road

*T*he photograph shows the Interurban Railroad car house and shops under construction sometime after February 1904. Shops were located at Sunol and San Carlos Streets. The new interurban cars were built by the American Car Company of St. Louis, Missouri and delivered in February 1904, thus helping to pinpoint a construction date.

The cars pictured in the photograph include the *Saratoga* (a trailer), the *Los Gatos* (a motor car), and line car #101. The hole in the foreground was the basement of the home of E.O. McGraff who sold the property to the Saratoga Construction Company. The house was cut in half and moved across San Carlos Street on rollers and set up on the northwest corner. The family continued to live there for many years. The Saratoga Construction Company became the San Jose and Los Gatos Interurban Railroad Company upon completion of construction.

New cars of the San Jose and Los Gatos Interurban R. R.

$\mathcal{G}$eorge Edwin Hyde was born January 1, 1855 in Benicia, California. He married Alice Louise Hill on August 15, 1878. After spending the early years of their marriage living in San Francisco and Benicia, the Hydes, in 1886, moved to this Saratoga house located on a 26 acre orchard on the north side of Prospect Road just east of Johnson Road.

The Shingle Style architecture illustrated here was popular, especially on the east coast, from about 1880 to 1900. A relatively simple style, shingle has been considered the first style in the modern tradition. It is characterized by unpainted wood shingles from the roof down to the foundation walls. In this instance river rock, possibly from nearby Quito-Campbell Creek, forms the foundation as well as the base of the porch pillars and fireplace.

According to Jeanette Watson's *Campbell, the Orchard City*, in 1909 George Hyde became the majority stockholder in the Campbell Fruit Growers Union. He changed the name of the packing and canning plant to the George E. Hyde Company and worked to modernize the industry. A cafeteria for his working crew and a day nursery for workers' children were among his accomplishments. Hyde was also an early director of the Campbell Water Company.

Residence of Geo. E. Hyde, on Interurban Road

*A*ccording to Thompson and West's 1876 *Historical Atlas Map of Santa Clara County California,*
"The soil of this County is varied, but in all of it variations it loses none of its excellence.
It is generally a loam made up of alluvial deposits, and ranges in depth from four feet to
an indefinite distance. In some portions of the valley it has been penetrated to a depth
of over a hundred feet, and the bottom was not found. Its adaptability to different prod-
ucts depends principally upon its proximity to water-courses. Most of it is easily
worked, and if ordinary care is used in its cultivation, yields bountiful harvests to the
husbandman."

Thompson and West continues, "Every variety of fruit known to the temperate zone
reaches the greatest perfection in this valley." Among the fruits grown in the valley were:
apples, peaches, pears, plums, cherries, nectarines, quinces, apricots, figs, lemons, oranges,
limes, pomelos, olives, prunes, mulberries, almonds, walnuts, and table and wine grapes.

Cultivating orchard in Winter on the line of the Interurban R. R.

$\mathcal{T}$his photograph of the tracks adjacent to Saratoga Avenue at Fruitdale Avenue near Congress Junction was probably taken late in 1903. The overhead wires had not yet been strung. Congress Junction was renamed Champagne Junction in the 1950's to acknowledge the Paul Masson Winery located nearby.

The storage tank on the right held water used to wet down the dusty county road. The boysen oak in the photograph stood until recently.

The carriage in the photograph is a surrey wagon, a truly American invention. Developed by the James Brewster Company of New York City in 1872, the surrey wagon combined the body of an English Whitechapel cart with the undercarriage of a road wagon.

The surrey had two sets of two forward-facing seats, the rear seats being removable. In its early days, one of the surrey's front seats could be pushed forward to allow access to the rear; later, the sides were cut down for easier entry. Another model of the surrey featured the cut under body which permitted the front wheels to turn sharply under the body of the carriage.

On the line of the San Jose and Los Gatos Interurban Road

The Sorosis Fruit Company on Saratoga Avenue once belonged to Francis Marion Smith, better known as "Borax" Smith after he made his first fortune with 20 mule teams in Death Valley's borax mines.

Smith, a multi-millionaire real estate developer, established a dehydrating and fruit packing plant on his 250 acre ranch, and had plans for extending the key system rail line which he fathered from the East Bay through Hayward to San Jose, Santa Clara, Saratoga, and Los Gatos. Smith died in 1931 without fulfilling his dream, but James Rea and F.S. Granger had long before grabbed off a piece of the dream when they constructed the interurban line from San Jose to Los Gatos and Saratoga in 1904.

Fred W. Crandall managed the Sorosis Fruit Company from the mid-1890's to about 1905. The ranch, which grew a variety of fruit, was located near where Mellon Drive and Saratoga Avenue intersect.

Orange Orchard, Sorosis Fruit Farm on the line of Interurban Road

*T*his photograph is of the construction phase of the San Jose and Los Gatos Interurban Railroad. Only the tracks have been laid. The location is between Saratoga and Bonnie Brae.

San Jose and Saratoga Road on the line of the San Jose and Los Gatos Interurban R. R.

The Bonnie Brae trestle paralleling Saratoga-Los Gatos Road is pictured here. The photograph was taken looking towards Los Gatos, during the construction phase of the Interurban Railroad project.

Trestle, on line of the San Jose and Los Gatos Interurban Road
On the line of the San Jose and Los Gatos Interurban R. R.

$\mathcal{L}$ooking east down Saratoga-Los Gatos Road (now Austin Way) near Austin Corners (Quito Road) in late 1903. The line poles on the ground are yet to be installed.

The community of Austin Corners was home to the Los Gatos and Saratoga Wine and Fruit Company Winery. A spur line of the Interurban Railroad was eventually built into the winery. The structure visible at the end of the track was a residence.

As of this date (1994), evidence of the rails still exists in the pavement at Austin and Quito Roads.

Between Los Gatos and Saratoga on the line of the S. J. L. G. and Saratoga Interurban Road

$\mathcal{S}$aratoga-Los Gatos Road at Daves Avenue between Austin Corners and the town of Los Gatos. Daves Avenue went under the railroad trestle. This construction photograph highlights the Santa Cruz Mountains in the background.

Trestle on the line of the S. J. & Los Gatos Interurban R. R. between Saratoga and Los Gatos

*S*ituated half-way between Saratoga and Los Gatos on the famous "Blossom Trolley Line", Nippon Mura Inn (Japanese Village) attained wide fame. Tourists from all parts of the world who visited the valley included Nippon Mura in their itinerary during the early 1900's.

With a comprehensive love of Japanese culture, Lucy and Theodore Morris, formerly of Yokahama, Japan, returned to California after thirty-four years with the China-Japan Trading Company. They purchased the 30 acre Miller Place in 1902 and transformed the property into a showplace using modified Japanese architecture. The Inn was furnished with exquisite Japanese furniture and rare curios and was enhanced by landscaped gardens of wisteria, cherry blossoms and crysanthemums.

Today the site is the La Hacienda Inn Hotel located at 18840 Saratoga-Los Gatos Road. Part of the original main building is incorporated into the restaurant.

Japanese Cottage at Nippon Mura, on line of the San Jose & Los Gatos Interurban R.R.

*B*y 1904 Los Gatos boasted that it had two banks, a post office, express telegraph and telephone offices, and a number of first-class hotels. Many of these commercial buildings can be seen in this photograph.

John Weldon Lyndon (1836-1913) was one of the pioneer builders of Los Gatos. A native of Vermont, Lyndon journeyed to California via the Isthmus of Panama and settled at Lexington in the Santa Cruz Mountains in 1859.

He purchased Los Gatos' first hotel, the Ten Mile House, at the corner of East Main Street and South Santa Cruz Avenue and the adjoining 100 acres for $7,500 from Henry D. McCobb in 1868. By 1889 the value of the land alone had climbed to $17,075. Lyndon subdivided his property when the Southern Pacific Railroad came into Los Gatos. His hotel, then known as the Los Gatos Hotel, was moved across the street to make way for the depot. The hotel experienced a fire in 1898, but was rebuilt. After the fire, the hotel was renamed the Lyndon Hotel and stood until the early 1960's.

When Los Gatos' Board of Trade (later the Chamber of Commerce) was organized on June 1, 1891, Lyndon was elected president. He founded the Bank of Los Gatos as well as the Los Gatos Gas Company and was a stockholder in the Los Gatos Fruit Packing Company.

Los Gatos on line of S. J. and Los Gatos Interurban R. R.

[Hotel Lyndon - center of photo]

$\mathcal{O}$ne of the many creeks that transversed the valley floor, possibly Los Gatos Creek. Note the wheel marks on the road where it came down to cross the creek. At the turn of the century there were not many bridges spanning the Valley's creeks.

Near line of the San Jose and Los Gatos Interurban R.R.

*R*ising above the towns of Los Gatos and Saratoga and bordering the Santa Clara Valley on the west side are the Santa Cruz Mountains. A paragraph from *Ten Years in Paradise* by Mary Bowden Carroll describes the mountains in the following manner:

> "On the west the Santa Cruz mountains, with their large and profitable vineyards, rise and shut out the winds from the ocean. In the recesses of these mountains is the home of that distinctively California tree, the redwood. There also are large oaks, madrones, sycamores, shrubs, and underbrush, which serve as a cover for various kinds of game; while in the wooded hills and ravines, hunting and angling can be enjoyed."

Andrew Hill's particular love and fascination was with the redwood trees. At the time of the Interurban Railroad construction project, Mr. Hill had already championed the redwood's cause by successfully lobbying for the passage of the California Redwood Park bill which created Big Basin Park. He continued the fight to save the Big Basin redwoods from logger's saws the rest of his life. Hill also continued to photograph the area until his death in 1922.

Mountain road to the heights, above the line of the San Jose and Los Gatos Interurban R. R.

The young lady in the photograph was Lorraine Figel. Born in 1892 she was the daughter of Fred and Grace (Roop) Figel of San Jose. Her father was manager of the Pacific Portland Cement Company. Her mother was a member of the Roop family, owners of Gilroy Hot Springs.

Lorraine Figel grew up in San Jose and at the time it is believed this photograph was taken (1904) lived at 561 South Fifth Street.

She married Raymond Johnston, a clerk in the Portland Cement Company, in 1912 or 1913. Records show Mrs. Johnston was living in Los Angeles in 1917. Lorraine later married Martin B. Miner of Santa Clara. Mr. and Mrs. Miner were living in Sacramento when Martin died in 1944.

Lorraine is buried in her family's plot in Oak Hill Memorial Park. At the time of her death, December 30, 1962, she was living in San Francisco. She was again a widow whose last name was Martin according to mortuary records.

The pony's name is unknown.

Miss Figel and her pony

$\mathscr{B}$otanists began categorizing Santa Clara Valley wildflowers more than 130 years ago. Rich in flora, the valley has over 1,000 varieties of wildflowers.

Many factors influence the numbers and kinds of wildflowers in an area. Climate, water, vegetation, and soil composition are among the most important. Another strong influence on the wildflower population is man. Humans both destroy and create wildflower environments. Development and land use changes can destroy wildflower habitats, and consequently the proliferation of flowers. At the same time new species of wildflowers can be introduced to a geographic area by migrating populations.

It is certain that the valley wildflower scene today is very different from that experienced by the Anza party in 1777. It is also true that the wildflower fields Andrew Hill enjoyed and photographed are unlike the ones we enjoy today.

California Wild flowers in the Santa Clara Valley near line of the S. J. & L. G. R. R.

*C*herry blossoms, photographed in the orchard of Harry Postlewaite, San Jose property owner and one-time associate of realtor T.S. Montgomery, are of the Cleveland Bigarreau variety.

Postlewaite, a native of England, was listed in the 1905 directory as a "country salesman" for Montgomery. He built a home on South Fourteenth Street and also owned an orange grove in Lindsey, California.

His daughter, Marjorie, violinist and sportswoman, was a tennis star in the 1920's and 30's. She died in 1948, and her father died the following year. Their home in their later years was at 1385 Hanchett Avenue.

NINE YEAR OLD ROYAL ANNE CHERRY TREE
ON ORCHARD OF H.P.OSTLETHWAITE NEAR SANTA CLARA.CAL.

*J*osephine Clifford McCrackin had, perhaps, almost as much to do with saving the redwoods in Big Basin as her long-time friend, Andrew P. Hill.

Mrs. McCrackin, poet and newspaperwoman, helped form the Sempervirens Club and her newspaper articles battling the Santa Cruz mountain's lumber industry went a long way in helping Hill create Big Basin State Park.

Her home high up on Loma Prieta Avenue was called Monte Paraiso. It was a mecca for California artists, musicians, and writers such as Bret Harte, Mark Twain, Ina Coolbrith, Joaquin Miller and Ambrose Bierce, before being destroyed in a forest fire in 1899. After the fire Mrs. McCrackin moved to Santa Cruz where she died in 1920.

The High Gate at Josephine Clifford McCrackin's home Santa Cruz
Mountains above line of the S. F. & L. G. S. V. R. R.

The three native varieties of oaks most prevalent in the Santa Clara Valley were the Coast Live Oak, an evergreen tree, and the Valley Oak and California White Oak, both deciduous trees. The Mediterranean climate of warm, dry summers and mild winters was conducive to the proliferation of these oaks. Seventy foot high oaks with an equal spread were a common sight to early settlers.

The "wild" native oaks on the valley floor are now an endangered species. Development and modern gardening methods have contributed to the mighty oak's demise. The soil condition known as oak root fungus, a residual effect of the oak forests, exists today in many Santa Clara Valley neighborhoods, a reminder of the magnificent oaks and their former presence in the valley.

Natural Oaks of the Valley and of S.S. & L.G. Interurban R.R.

$\mathscr{O}$rchards began coming into production in the 1880's and as early as 1891 fruit growers formed associations that helped grade and market their crops.

In 1900, there were 4,788,615 orchard trees in the valley equating to approximately 41,000 acres of orchards, and by 1915 the valley was producing one-third of the world's prunes. In 1925, farming in Santa Clara Valley reached its peak; there were 6,959 farms in operation at that time.

Farm land at the turn of the century sold for $75 - $600 per acre depending on its proximity to San Jose.

An old farm, entrance, as the valley looked before the fruit industry commenced.
On line of the S. J. & L. G. I. R. R.

C.C. Morse was called the "Seed King of America."

Charles Copeland Morse gave his name to a company known to home and commercial gardeners here and in 100 other countries.

C.C. Morse was a Maine farm boy who went to sea at age seventeen, then mined for silver in Virginia City's Comstock strike, and finally bought a Santa Clara seed business in 1877. Morse and his partner L.A. Kellogg, a Methodist minister, scraped up $20,000 to buy the seed-growing company of R.W. Wilson who owned land near the Santa Clara railroad depot.

In 1884 Morse bought out Kellogg and took his son, Lester L. Morse, into the business. Lester was still attending Santa Clara Grammar School at the time. Morse & Co. began acquiring additional property around Sunnyvale and Lawrence Station, then in the Gilroy area. Morse died in 1900 and his son carried on. In 1930 the firm merged with another old seed business, D.M. Ferry & Co.

Some miles of seed farming. Santa Clara Valley near Santa Clara. S. J. & L. G. I. R. R.

At the turn of the century Santa Clara County was one of the largest seed-growing areas in the world. The long growing season allowed the seeds maximum time to ripen. In addition to flowers, there were fields of onion, lettuce, and other vegetables covering hundreds of acres. Leeks, standing higher than a man's head, produced fields of vivid purple blossoms. This photograph was taken on the C.C. Morse and Company's great Santa Clara seed farm.

According to *Sunshine, Fruit and FIowers,* published in 1895 and 1896, "all the seeds are gathered by hand, and spread on canvas sheets to dry, after which they are thrashed with flails by hand, or with machines made especially for the purpose."

Onion field near San Jose, Santa Clara Valley S. J. & L. G. R. R.

*G*rape vines bowed to the ground with the luxuriance and weight of the delicious fruit. To obtain the greatest financial return, the grape grower had to convert his product into wine. By the 1880's wine became so popular in the valley that almost every homeowner who raised grapes either as a major crop or for personal use, made wine for his family's consumption.

Some of the grapes were processed at the Los Gatos and Saratoga Wine and Fruit Winery at Austin Corners between Saratoga and Los Gatos. Processing at the winery began in 1885 and continued until prohibition went into effect.

In the vineyard, gathering grapes, showing yield on S. J. & L. G. I. R. R.

*O*ne of the most popular flowers grown on Santa Clara Valley seed farms was the sweet pea. At the turn of the century more than ninety varieties of sweet peas were being cultivated, including a dwarf white "pea" known as "Cupid." Artesian wells throughout the Santa Clara Valley provided irrigation, which in addition to the warm sunshine and rich soil, made this a premiere area for producing vegetable and flower seeds.

Field of Peas in Blossom near line of S. J. & L. G. R. R.

In 1900 there were 525,030 apricot trees in the Santa Clara Valley. By 1925, California produced 96% of the apricots nationwide.

The variety of apricot most abundant in the Santa Clara Valley was the Blenheim apricot. The Blenheim was developed in Britain in 1830.

Valley apricots were canned, dried, and sold for consumption. An early bloomer (June/July), Blenheims could safely be kept for two weeks after harvesting. If the fruit was to be canned, it was picked when firm ripe and before it attained apricot color. Although susceptible to brown rot, apricots grown in the valley did not exhibit this disease because of the dry springs and summers.

Picking apricots near line of S. J. & L. G. R. R. Co.

$\mathscr{F}$ields were tilled in the spring, and up to ten times during the growing season, to kill weeds and aerate the soil. Orchardists did not want the weeds competing with the trees for water, a precious commodity. Water for the trees came from three sources: nearby streams, artesian springs, or underground wells.

Tilling could be contracted out. In the 1890's shallow tilling cost $2.00 per acre; deep tilling $3.00 per acre. Contracts for plowing, harrowing and pruning ran between $7.50 - $10 per acre.

Festivals celebrating spring and the life of the orchards were held in almost every community in the valley. The San Jose Blossom Festival was one of the largest spring festivals.

Tilling an orchard in Springtime. Taken near line of the S. J. L. G. Interurban R. R.

In 1891 a group of Santa Clara Valley fruit growers formed the West Side Growers' Association with the objective of securing more economical means of drying their fruit and better methods of marketing their product. The success of this Association led to the establishment of the Campbell Fruit Growers Union the following year.

Participation in the Union provided individual growers with the collective advantages of more uniform and cheaper grading of their fruit, and better prices for their product. The Union advertised the fruits effectively to increase demand for the product and supplied the market carefully to avoid over-supply.

A drying ground West Side District near line of S. J. & L. G. Interurban R. R.

*P*rofessor Charles W. Childs (1844-1922) was born in Geneseo, New York, and came to Placerville in 1861. He graduated from the State Normal School in San Francisco in 1867. In 1878, after that institution had moved to San Jose, he joined its faculty to head the history, civil government and bookkeeping departments. After being named vice-principal in 1886, Childs served as principal (the title was later changed to president) from 1889-1896. He was the first graduate of the Normal School to become its principal. He was elected president of the California Teachers Association in 1898.

Childs lived on Almaden Road: the *1893 San Jose City Directory* lists his residence address as "four miles out." Although he grew prunes on the forty acres adjacent to his home, it is believed that this picture was of his other property.

Pen Pictures of the Garden of the World by H.S. Foote describes this land as follows:

"Mr. Childs also owns, on Stevens Creek, in the Lincoln District, a fine orchard property of 25 acres, the trees now (1888) being six years old and in splendid condition. Two-thirds of that orchard is in prunes and one-third in peaches. The Professor also engages in fruit-drying. Of the crop in 1887, he cured about 120 tons and expects this year to handle about 250 tons."

Childs left the Normal School after a dispute with Governor James H. Budd and was employed with the Oakland schools from 1909-1916. Later he became an orchardist with holdings in Vacaville, St. Helena, and Strathmore.

Drying grounds of Prof. Childs showing the partial crop of prunes of one farm.
S. J. L. G. Interurban Road

The son of a pioneer foundry owner, Joseph G. Enright worked in his father's foundry building farm equipment and the famous Enright's Patent Strawburning Portable Engine invented by the elder Enright. The engine was California's first portable engine used for threshing wheat and was sold throughout the state wherever grain was grown.

Joseph Enright entered the real estate field during the boom years of the 1890's after his father retired from the foundry business.

When Enright died in 1905 at age 39, he was living in the family home at William and Clay (later 19th) Streets on Coyote Creek in east San Jose.

Jos. G. Enright home orchard. S. J. L. G. Interurban Rail Road

According to Sunshine, Fruit and Flowers, olive trees were first introduced to the Santa Clara Valley by the Franciscan fathers at the Santa Clara Mission. The climate and soil of the valley were exceptionally suited to their cultivation.

The first olive grove of significance was planted by Don Jose Arguello on his Quito rancho. The trees were of the Mission variety. The El Quito farm, later owned by E.E. Goodrich, boasted 3,800 olive trees at the turn of the century. Olive oil was the principal product, valuable both as a food and as medicine.

Quito Olive Farm near the line of San Jose and Los Gatos Interurban Rail Road

$\mathscr{P}$rior to the mid-nineteenth century what is now called Los Gatos Creek was known variously as Arroyo Temporal de la Majonera (the Story Landmark River), Arroyo del Rancho, Arroyo de Los Gatos, and Jones Creek (after Zachariah Jones).

The Los Gatos Creek drains a large part of the watershed of the Santa Cruz Mountain and constitutes the official line of division of those mountains between the Sierra Morena (the dark mountains) on the south and the Sierra Azule (the blue mountains) to the north.

The creekbed enters Los Gatos, running under the Main Street bridge. Here was once located the so-called Hangman's bridge from which a member of Tibercio Vasquez's gang was reputedly hanged. The original Main Street bridge was first built in 1858 and rebuilt after the floods of 1862 and 1872. In 1906 the Town of Los Gatos and the San Jose & Los Gatos Interurban Railway Company shared expenses to build a stone and concrete three-arched bridge for the interurban's Campbell cutoff track to San Jose.

Between 1855 and 1887 the waters of Los Gatos Creek provided power for the operation of James Alexander Forbes' Santa Rosa Brand Flour Mill, later called the Los Gatos Manufacturing Company. In 1868 the San Jose Water Company took the water from the mill race and built a flume and reservoirs to provide water for San Jose.

Dry Creek Road, which runs between Union and Hicks Avenues in Willow Glen, was once a part of Los Gatos Creek; the flood of December 20, 1866 caused a permanent change of course.

Los Gatos Creek S. J. L. G. Interurban Road

The community of Gilroy, in southern Santa Clara County, is named after the Scotsman John Gilroy who arrived in California in 1814 and became its first non-Hispanic citizen. The town is situated in the center of a valley about eight miles wide and twenty miles long. The foothills of the Coast Range rise to the east and northeast of Gilroy and to the northwest lies a section of the Santa Cruz Range.

This photograph shows the level and fertile valley which was watered by the Uvas, Llagas, San Felipe, and Pajaro Rivers. It was planted extensively in grain and was home to a large dairy industry. Gilroy's principal product at the turn of the century was cheese.

Santa Clara Valley near Gilroy

William Fisher first saw California in 1820 as a cabin boy on a New England clipper ship seeking hides and tallow. In 1845 he returned and fell in love with the beautiful and fertile Santa Clara Valley.

For an astonishingly high bid of $6,000 Fisher purchased the 23,000 acre Rancho Laguna Seca from Juan Alvirez in 1845. Rancho Laguna Seca was an old Spanish land grant ordered sold by the courts. It was located twelve miles south of San Jose and boasted rich agricultural land and grand old oaks. Fisher planted extensive orchards and vineyards and raised large herds of cattle on his property.

Mrs. Mary Murphy Colombet, one of Fisher's daughters, still retained almost 4,500 acres of the old rancho at the turn of the century when this photograph was taken.

A combined harvester. On the Murphy Ranch Santa Clara Valley.

*I*n addition to his photography business, located in downtown San Jose in the Porter block, Andrew P. Hill conducted a poultry brokerage with partner William H. Yeats at 313 Willow Street. There they bought and sold fancy poultry, including Black Spanish and Plymouth Rocks. The Plymouth Rocks were probably raised for both their eggs and meat.

A finely bred yard of Barred Plymouth Rockes. Owned by Andrew P. Hill, San Jose, California.
One year old weight of hen average 8-1/4 pounds. Cock 12 pounds

$\mathcal{R}$ancho Milpitas, a 4,000+ acre ranch extending eastward from Milpitas Road to the hills above Piedmont Road and southward from Calaveras Road to Cropley Avenue was granted to Nicolas Berreyesa (historic spelling) in 1834 by the alcalde of San Jose. The granting was disputed by Jose Maria Alviso. In 1835, Governor Castro re-granted the land to Alviso.

Rincon de los Esteros, a 6,000+ acre rancho which encompassed the land east of the Guadalupe River near Alviso to the outskirts of Milpitas was granted to Ygnacio Alviso in 1838 by Governor Alvarado. The United States later declared that 1,800 acres of Rincon de los Esteros be granted to Francisco Berreyesa.

Far to the south, in the New Almaden and Calero area, Governor Alvarado granted 4,000+ acres to Jose de los Reyes Berreyesa in 1842. Litigation over the title consumed two decades because the Almaden Quicksilver Mining Company also laid claim to the land. The dispute was settled in favor of Berreyesa's heirs in 1868.

Both this photograph and the photograph on the next page appear to have been taken on the Rincon de los Esteros land.

Ruins of the Old Berryessa House. One of the first houses built in Santa Clara Valley

*A*dobe missions, residences, and municipal buildings dotted the California landscape from the beginning of the Spanish colonization period. Adobe structures were constructed of blocks of sun dried clay and straw. Additional clay was used as mortar between the bricks to reinforce the structure, and wooden beams were used above the doors and windows to stabilize the openings. If properly cared for, adobe is a very lasting building material. Adobe is also an excellent insulator; heat is retained in the winter and repelled in the summer.

The first floor of an adobe had packed dirt floors and was usually divided into two rooms, the *sala* (living room), and the *recamara* (bedroom). The second floor of an adobe was used as a sleeping loft. Windows and doors were covered with curtains, animal hides, or wood shutters.

Most activities of the early settlers took place outside the adobes, either on the veranda or in the hacienda yards. Because of San Jose's mild climate, most of the cooking and socializing was done out-of-doors year round. The adobes themselves were used mainly for sleeping and escaping inclement weather.

Adobe house on the Berryessa Place. One of the first built in the county near San Jose, Cal

The Pajaro River begins at the San Felipe Lake (called "Soap Lake" by the locals). Wandering down through the Gabilan Mountain Range by way of Chittenden Pass, the river first serves as the boundary between Santa Clara and San Benito counties and, lower, between the counties of Santa Cruz and Monterey.

The history of the Pajaro River is recorded in the diary of Father Juan Crespi, a member of the expedition of Don Gaspar de Portola. On October 7, 1769 the group came upon a river. At its edge had been left as an offering ..."a bird which the heathen had killed and stuffed with straw." For this reason Portola's soldiers called the stream Rio de Pajaro (River of the Bird).

The name Pajaro stuck despite the fact that the expressed preference of the priests in the party was for the name Santa Ana, and that in some old records appears the name Rio de los Paxaros after the number of ducks in the area.

According to *Sunshine, Fruit and Flowers*, this picture of the river was taken near Sargents Station: "The river at this point flows very gently, and the overhanging trees and windings of the river make the river scenery very beautiful. The river can be navigated with row boats a distance of two miles below the station, and this feature is an attractive one to the campers. Fish are very plentiful, as the stream flows into the ocean, and the supply of certain varieties is inexhaustible."

Sargents Station was a small community and shipping point named after J.P. Sargent. It was located on the Pajaro River five miles from Gilroy. It was a popular picnic resort at the turn of the century and a destination point for hunters, fishermen, bicycle clubs, and other San Jose and San Francisco social groups on outings.

Pajaro River

The Saratoga Hotel built in the 1880's, was located on Lumber Street (Big Basin Way) near Third Street and was patterned after the Saratoga Hotel, Saratoga Springs, New York.

This, however, is a photograph of the flower gardens in front of the hotel at Pacific Congress Springs, a resort located in the Santa Cruz mountains about five miles from Los Gatos.

In the early 1860's mineral waters above Saratoga were discovered to have nearly the same chemical content as the celebrated spa at Saratoga Springs, New York. Capitalists Darius Mills and Alvinza Hayward purchased the 720 acres in 1864 for a reported $2,000 and developed the springs into a fashionable and popular resort, Pacific Congress Springs.

In 1866 the elegant Congress Hall Hotel was built on a protected plateau on the mountainside. It consisted of about 100 rooms, all of which opened onto a veranda, and attracted worldwide patronage until the turn of the century.

Unfortunately, the hotel was destroyed by fire in 1903 and heavy financial losses cancelled plans to rebuild. Only a combined restaurant and clubhouse, with adjacent picnic grounds, were developed for social festivities.

Flowers in front of Saratoga Hotel Saratoga Springs near the S. J. & L. G. Interurban line

Eschscholzia california was named for a Russian ship's surgeon, Johan Friedrich Gustav von Eschscholtz, a young doctor from the Baltic port of Dorpat. The ship, *Rurik*, on a journey to find the Northwest Passage, sailed into San Francisco Bay in 1817 for provisions and to assess the strength of the Spanish forces at the San Francisco Presidio. While docked, a young botanist on board, Adelbert von Charmisso, and Eschscholtz went ashore and discovered the orange wildflower. Charmisso honored his friend Eschscholtz by naming the poppy after him.

Gold miners, forty years later, found symbolism in the golden flower and pressed the poppies to include in their letters back home.

The California legislature granted *Eschscholzia california* official state flower status in 1903.

Eschscholtzia or California poppy. Indigenous to Cal. Growing along the line of the Interurban Road

In 1900 there were 127,165 cherry trees in the Santa Clara Valley.

Cherry blossoms are probably the loveliest of all fruit blossoms. There are over 600 varieties of cherries, both sweet and sour. Cherries in the Bigarreau group are of the sweet variety. The most notable Bigarreau cherry is the Bing cherry.

Cherry blossom spring festivals are held throughout the world. The most famous are those in Japan and Washington D.C.

Cherry Blossoms

The name Century plant is a misnomer since the plant actually blossoms after approximately ten years. A Mexican species of the *agave* plant, the branched flower stalk of the Century plant can range in height from 15-40 feet.

The two women in the photograph are dressed in the fashion of the day. The woman on the right is dressed in a striped afternoon dress. Her visitor (wearing a straw boater hat and carrying a reticule) is dressed in a walking skirt, topped by a high collared, leg-a-mutton sleeved blouse. Their attire suggests it is spring or summer.

The Century Plant. Along the line of the Interurban Road

$\mathcal{T}$he palms in the photograph appear to be *Washingtonia Filifera* palms which are native to California. They grow as tall as 75 feet. The thick, shag-covered trunk palms rise to an open crown of large, fan-shaped leaves which at first stand erect, then droop gradually, and finally die and rest like a brown thatch skirt around the trunk. The shag is left on the tree for appearance.

This palm, because of its size, is used most often in large gardens. These impressive trees were and are still used to line driveways and wide streets.

The palms do flower and some trees set fruit. The fruit is edible and was used by Native Americans for food.

A garden on the S. L. & L. G. Interurban Road

Although Andrew Hill titled this photograph "Branding calves near San Jose and Los Gatos Interurban Rail Road," according to *Sunshine, Fruit and Flowers* the photograph was taken at the J.P. Sargent Ranch below Gilroy.

Sada S. Coe in her book *The Lost Trails* describes a day of branding at the Sargent Ranch as follows: "...we pushed our horses to a fast trot on down the highway 101 to the Sargent ranch where the foreman and his wife were just finishing breakfast. We had coffee with them and rested our horses for a time, then they saddled their mounts and we were off to the branding.

"Five hundred head of big black Pole Angus calves were bawling for their mothers in the large round corral. The branding fires were burning and the irons getting hot, while the ropers tightened their saddles and waited for their place in the corral. Only four ropers at a time were allowed in the corral, and each rider waited his turn near the branding fire until the boss sent him in to catch a calf and the other roper to come out to rest his horse. So all of us roped calves until the daylight hours faded into dusk, and finally the last calf was branded. The gates of the corral were opened, and the five hundred bawling babies were turned out to their anxious mothers peering at them through the fence.

"Suddenly everything was very quiet. Tired horses and men stood silently around the dying embers of the branding fire. It had been a real day's work, but for us, there was yet the long forty mile ride home. We rode back to Sargent Ranch, fed and rested our horses, while someone cooked a bit of dinner and we ate. It was our first food since the night before."

Branding Calves near San Jose and Los Gatos Interurban R.R.

At the turn of the century there were approximately 25,000 head of cattle in Santa Clara County. Most of the range land was on the slopes of Mt. Hamilton or on land south of San Jose.

Cattle were evident in the valley since the early Spanish period. The Spanish mission fathers raised them and under Mexican rule, hides and tallow became the medium of exchange with foreign traders. During the Mexican period meat from the cattle was rarely eaten. It was not until the Gold Rush that cattle were valued for their meat.

Andrew P. Hill used cattle as the subject for several of his paintings and many of his photographs.

Cattle

$\mathcal{R}$ows of trees were often planted to form canopies over the roadways. These rows of eucalyptus trees may have been along Brokaw Road.

Blue gum eucalyptus trees were imported from Australia in the 1850's. The wood from the trees was called "iron wood" because it was so hard. Attempts were made to use it for railroad ties, but this proved unsuccessful because the wood split so easily. Only one man in the area, Thomas Gillespie, seemed to be able to work with the wood successfully. He had a mill on San Fernando Street.

Along the line of the San Jose and Los Gatos Interurban Road

$\mathcal{T}$he first comprehensive survey of the corporate limits of the City of San Jose was done in 1850. The city boundaries were roughly Coyote Creek, Rosa (Hedding) Street, the Guadalupe River, and Alma Street. As development occurred, previously surveyed streets were named by either the property developers or city surveyors.

Newspaperman Hugh De Lacy was responsible for the street number system in San Jose. First and Santa Clara Streets became the central point of the numbering system instituted in 1884.

The first street to be paved in San Jose was First Street between Santa Clara and San Salvador Streets in 1890. The City financed the paving with the proceeds from a public improvements bond sale. Many of San Jose's streets remained unpaved well into the twentieth century.

Avenue near San Jose